I'M ALLERGIC TO... Eggs

Written by E.C. Andrews

Published in 2025 by
KidHaven Publishing, an Imprint of
Greenhaven Publishing, LLC
2544 Clinton St., Buffalo, NY 14224

© 2024 BookLife Publishing Ltd.

Written by: E.C. Andrews
Edited by: Rebecca Phillips-Bartlett
Designed by: Jasmine Pointer

All facts, statistics, web addresses and URLs in this book were verified as valid and accurate at time of writing. No responsibility for any changes to external websites or references can be accepted by either the author or publisher.

Cataloging-in-Publication Data

Names: Andrews, E.C.
Title: Eggs / E.C. Andrews.
Description: Buffalo, NY : KidHaven Publishing, 2025. | Series: I'm allergic to… | Includes glossary and index.
Identifiers: ISBN 9781534549043 (pbk.) | ISBN 9781534549050 (library bound) | ISBN 9781534549067 (ebook)
Subjects: LCSH: Food allergy in children--Juvenile literature. | Eggs as food--Juvenile literature. | Allergy--Juvenile literature.
Classification: LCC RJ386.5 A53 2025 | DDC 616.97'5--dc23

All rights reserved.

No part of this book may be reproduced in any form without permission in writing from the publisher, except by a reviewer.

Manufactured in the United States of America

CPSIA compliance information: Batch #CW25KH
For further information contact Greenhaven Publishing LLC at 1-844-317-7404.

Please visit our website, www.greenhavenpublishing.com. For a free color catalog of all our high-quality books, call toll free 1-844-317-7404 or fax 1-844-317-7405.

Find us on

Image Credits

All images are courtesy of Shutterstock.com. With thanks to Getty Images, Thinkstock Photo and iStockphoto.
Cover – Lana Smirnova, fizkes, Vladislav Noseek, Africa Studio, Love the wind, Alter-ego, Joe Gough, Naddya, OlgaChernyak, stocksolutions, Volha Shaukavets. Throughout – Lana Smirnova. 4–5 – marilyn barbone, Photoroyalty. 6–7 – maxim ibragimov, Pearl PhotoPix. 8–9 – yarm_sasha, virtu studio, Nattika, zcw. 10–11 – gowithstock, MaraZe, Sarii Iuliia, Nattika, bonchan, Peter Hermes Furian, kanta_kulat. 12–13 – marishkaSm, Keith Homan. 14–15 – Nina Firsova, Moving Moment, scott conner. 16–17 – Tatjana Baibakova, Viktor1, Marian Weyo, Moving Moment, urfin. 18–19 – Nataly Studio, Anton Starikov, MIA Studio, Mr Max. 20–21 – Anna Pecherskaia, Africa Studio, Jiri Hera, iprachenko, Photoongraphy. 22–23 – takayuki, Rawpixel.com.

Contents

Page 4 — Delicious Diets

Page 6 — What Is an Allergy?

Page 8 — What Are Eggs?

Page 10 — What Are Egg Products?

Page 12 — Symptoms of an Egg Allergy

Page 14 — Smart Swaps

Page 16 — Perfect Protein

Page 18 — Super Salmon Bites

Page 20 — Eggless Pancakes

Page 22 — Allergies and Us

Page 24 — Glossary and Index

Words that look like **THIS** can be found in the glossary on page 24.

Delicious Diets

Our diet is made up of all the things we usually eat. We need to eat different types of foods to stay healthy. This is called eating a balanced diet.

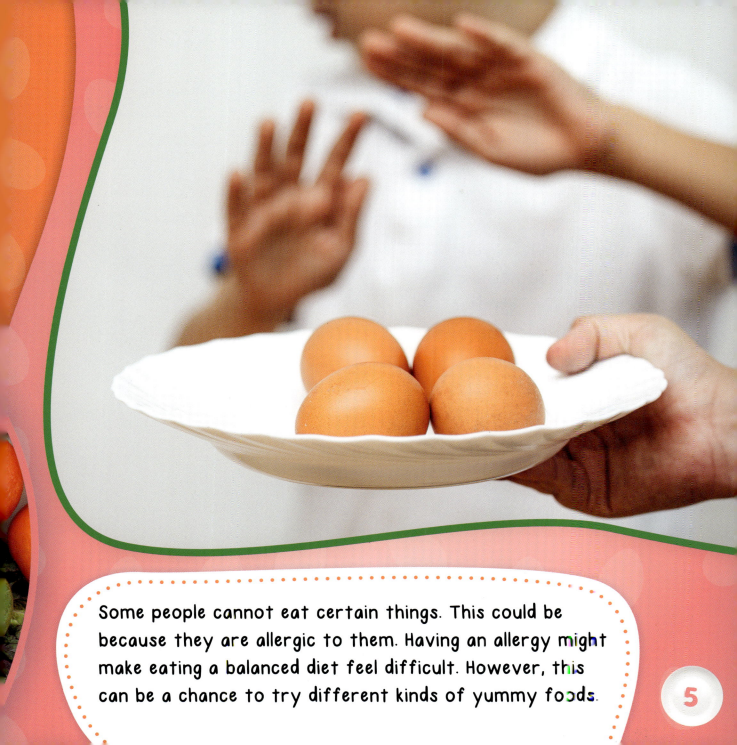

Some people cannot eat certain things. This could be because they are allergic to them. Having an allergy might make eating a balanced diet feel difficult. However, this can be a chance to try different kinds of yummy foods.

What Is an Allergy?

An allergy is when your body treats something that is usually harmless as though it is dangerous. This can cause your body to have an allergic **REACTION** when you eat or touch the thing you are allergic to.

Humans often eat chicken eggs, quail eggs, and duck eggs. Other types of eggs are eaten all over the world. However, chicken eggs are the most common.

Quail eggs

Duck eggs

What Are Egg Products?

Eggs can be eaten on their own. Eggs are also used as an **INGREDIENT** in other foods. Eggs are often found in these foods:

Noodles and pasta

Baked foods, such as cakes and cookies

Sauces, such as mayonnaise and hollandaise

10

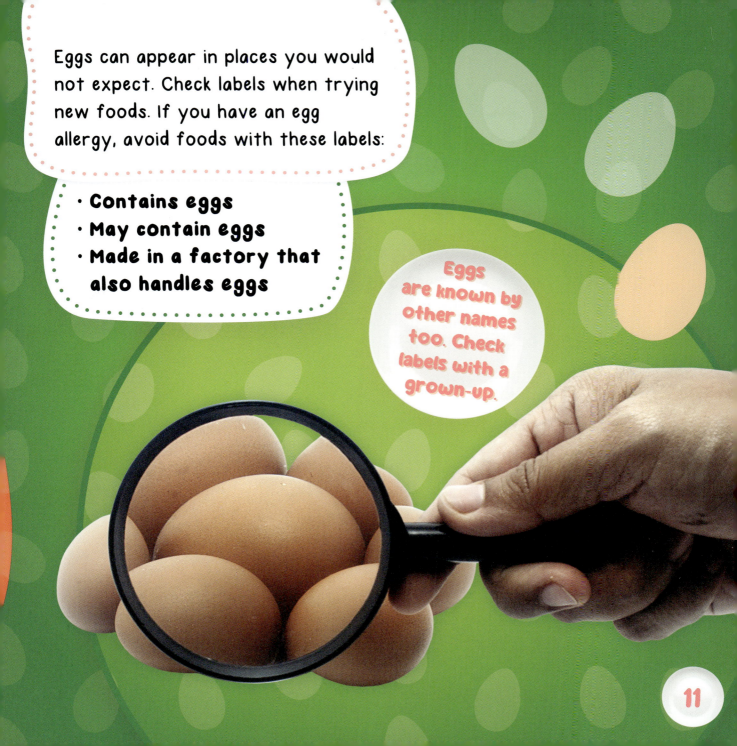

Symptoms of an
Egg Allergy

If you feel unwell after eating eggs, tell a grown-up. Egg allergies can cause these **SYMPTOMS**:

- **SWOLLEN** or itchy skin
- **Blocked nose**
- **Feeling or being sick**
- **Coughing**
- **Tight feeling in the chest**
- **Finding it difficult to breathe**

Anaphylaxis is an allergic reaction that is very dangerous. Autoinjectors **INJECT** medicine into your body that can help with anaphylaxis. If you have been given an autoinjector for your allergy, always keep it with you.

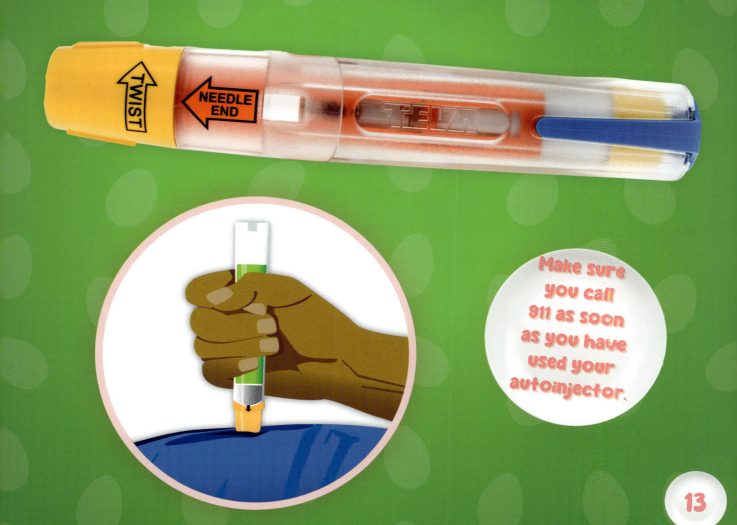

Make sure you call 911 as soon as you have used your autoinjector.

Smart Swaps

Whether they are scrambled, boiled, or fried, people often eat eggs at breakfast. However, a tofu scramble can be just as yummy. You can add other things to it, such as spinach and herbs.

A tofu scramble is great on toast!

When baking things such as cakes, eggs are often used to thicken the mixture and hold everything together. However, you can also use applesauce or mashed banana instead. These will also add extra **FLAVOR**.

Applesauce

Mashed banana

Perfect Protein

Eggs are often eaten as a **SOURCE** of protein. Protein helps your body grow strong and stay healthy. It is an important part of a balanced diet. However, you can find plenty of protein in other foods.

Broccoli, kidney beans, soybeans, nuts, and chickpeas are healthy sources of protein. Protein can also be found in dairy products, such as milk and cheese. Meat and fish can be healthy protein sources too.

Chickpeas

Turkey

Milk and cheese

Salmon

These foods can be used in lots of yummy RECIPES.

17

Super Salmon Bites

To make some super simple eggless salmon nuggets, you will need:

- Small pieces of salmon
- Flour
- A glass of milk
- Salt and pepper
- Egg-free breadcrumbs – remember to check the labels!

Salmon

Flour

Egg-free breadcrumbs

18

Let's cook!

- Preheat your oven to 350 degrees Fahrenheit (180 degrees Celsius).
- Brush your salmon pieces with milk.
- Put your flour, salt, and pepper into a bowl. Roll small pieces of salmon in the flour.
- Roll your salmon pieces in the egg-free breadcrumbs.
- Bake your salmon pieces in the oven until they are golden brown on the outside and the fish inside is flaky.

Eggless Pancakes

To make some yummy eggless pancakes, you will need:

- 1/2 cup of flour
- 10 ounces of milk
- 2 tablespoons of coconut oil

Flour

Coconut Oil

Milk

Let's cook!

- Put your flour and milk into a blender.
- Blend them into a smooth mixture.
- Brush the frying pan with coconut oil and heat it up. (Have a grown-up help!)
- Pour in a small amount of the mixture.
- After one to two minutes, flip the pancake with a spatula.
- Cook until both sides are golden.
- Enjoy with your favorite toppings!

Allergies and Us

Finding out that you have an egg allergy might make you feel worried about what you can and cannot eat. However, there are lots of ways to keep enjoying a delicious balanced diet.

Which egg-free recipe do you want to make?

This is a chance to get more adventurous in the kitchen! Just remember to be careful when you eat out and always check food labels. If you are not sure, ask a grown-up.

Glossary

flavor   how something tastes

ingredient   a food item that is combined with other foods to make a particular dish

inject   to push a liquid into something using a needlelike object

invertebrates   animals that do not have a backbone

reaction   something done or felt in response to something else

recipes   instructions explaining how to make certain foods or dishes

source   where something comes from

swollen   when something has become bigger than normal

symptoms   signs of an illness that can be used to tell what is wrong with someone

Index

allergies 5–8, 11–13, 22

cakes 10, 15, 20–21

diets 4–5, 16, 22

fish 8, 17, 19

flour 18–21

foods 4–5, 10–11, 16–17, 23

labels 11, 18, 23

salmon 17–19

sauces 10, 15